What's the Deal with Voting?

Ben Nussbaum

Reader Consultants

Brian Allman, M.A.
Classroom Teacher, West Virginia

Cynthia Donovan
Classroom Teacher, California

iCivics Consultants

Emma Humphries, Ph.D.
Chief Education Officer

Taylor Davis, M.T.
Director of Curriculum and Content

Natacha Scott, MAT
Director of Educator Engagement

Publishing Credits

Rachelle Cracchiolo, M.S.Ed., *Publisher*
Emily R. Smith, M.A.Ed., *VP of Content Development*
Véronique Bos, *Creative Director*
Dona Herweck Rice, *Senior Content Manager*
Dani Neiley, *Associate Editor*
Fabiola Sepulveda, *Series Designer*

Image Credits: p4 RBM Vintage Images/Alamy Stock Photo; p5 Shutterstock/noamgalai; p10 Library of Congress [LC-DIG-ppmsca-31598]; p11 Library of Congress [LC-DIG-ppmsca-58269]; p12 top Alamy/CPA Media Pte Ltd; p12 bottom Seattle Post-Intelligencer Collection, Museum of History & Industry, Seattle; All Rights Reserved; p13 Shutterstock/Joa Souza; p14 top Shutterstock/Photo-Denver; p14 bottom Shutterstock/Evgenia Parajanian; p15 Alamy/Bob Daemmrich; p16 Alamy/Zume Press Inc; p18 Alamy/Reuters; p19 Alamy/SOPA Images Limited; p20 top Getty Images/George Frey/Stringer; p20 bottom Shutterstock/Joseph Sohm; p21 Alamy/Lori Epstein; p23 Yin Bogu/Xinhua News; p24 Shutterstock/Jonathan Weiss; p26 Elkanah Tisdale (1771-1835); p27 Getty Images/NurPhoto; p29 top Alamy/Imago History Collection; p29 bottom Alamy/Storms Media Group; all other images from iStock and/or Shutterstock

TCM Teacher Created Materials
5482 Argosy Avenue
Huntington Beach, CA 92649
www.tcmpub.com

ISBN 978-1-0876-1541-7

Printed by: 51497
Printed in: Taiwan

Table of Contents

A Vote, a Voice

In the United States, people vote to decide who will lead their government. They vote on **issues**, too. They vote for presidents, **sheriffs**, mayors, members of the school board, and more. Every community has a voice. Every voter has a choice.

Voting is a way to make sure that the government works for the people. If leaders do not do their jobs well, they may lose their elections. New leaders may take their places. Being a responsible, informed voter is a way to make a community better.

There are many different types of ballots and ways to vote.

Each voter is allowed privacy to cast their vote.

Voting is at the very center of what the United States is all about. But what it means to vote is always changing. Some people have had to fight to be able to vote. Some people are still fighting today.

The tools people use to vote change as well. People can now vote in many different ways. They might vote by pushing a button on a screen, filling in a bubble, or writing down a name. Voting **differs** in different communities.

What is the fairest way to vote? What is the best way to vote? These are important questions with important answers. In the end, voting is a very big deal. In a **democracy** like the United States has, voting and voters matter.

Jump into Fiction

The Team Captain

Roberto and David are twins who play on a soccer team together. After practice one day, Coach Wilson gathers the team in a circle. "You need to pick a captain," he tells the players.

"The captain should be someone responsible. It's their job to talk to me about what you're all thinking. During the game, it's their job to talk to the referee," Coach Wilson says. "The captain is very important."

"Each of you write one name on a piece of paper," he continues. "Fold the paper in half, and then put it in my hat."

Roberto thinks for a little bit. He makes up his mind and votes for David, writing his brother's name on the paper.

David thinks for a little bit, too. He then votes for Roberto.

Soon, Coach Wilson's hat is filled with strips of paper that are folded in half. He pulls out his notebook and starts to tally the votes.

"Here are the results so far," he announces. "Jaime has five votes." Everyone looks at Jaime, a tall boy who plays goalkeeper for the team. "Roberto has four votes," Coach Wilson continues, "and David has three votes."

"I can't read someone's writing," Coach Wilson says, holding up a piece of paper that has a scribble on it. "That's mine," says a girl named Ella. Everyone looks at her as she says, "I voted for David."

"Okay," Coach Wilson says, taking the last piece of paper from his hat. "Someone else wrote Roberto and David. That vote isn't allowed since you had to select one person."

"That's my vote," says Gina. "Can I vote again?"

Before Coach Wilson can reply, another girl asks, "Jackson's not at practice today. Doesn't he get to vote?"

"Wait a minute," Roberto exclaims. "I think you have 14 slips of paper, but 15 players are here today."

Coach Wilson laughs. "I never knew voting could be so hard!" he says.

Back to Nonfiction

Who Gets to Vote?

Most people know that George Washington was the first president. But they may not know that very few people voted in that first U.S. election.

In most states, Black people could not vote. And in all states except one, women could not vote. Some states even had rules about what religion people had to belong to. In some states, no one voted. Instead, the leaders of the state decided that the state would support Washington.

HARPER'S WEEKLY.
A JOURNAL OF CIVILIZATION.

Vol. XI.—No. 568.] NEW YORK, SATURDAY, NOVEMBER 16, 1867. [SINGLE COPIES TEN CENTS. $4.00 PER YEAR IN ADVANCE.

Men of all races got the right to vote in 1870.

Brave Women Led the Way

Women who fought for the right to vote were often made fun of and criticized. They were even beaten, threatened, and jailed. This was done to intimidate them and get them to stop fighting for their rights. Susan B. Anthony (right), Elizabeth Cady Stanton, Ida B. Wells, and Alice Paul were some of these brave leaders.

Over time, more and more people have won the right to vote. The government helps protect those rights thanks to **amendments**.

The 15th Amendment to the **Constitution** gave Black men the right to vote. The 19th Amendment gave women that right. These were huge changes. Many people fought against these changes. They wanted things to stay the way they were.

Today, most people agree that voting is important. They also agree that most people should be able to vote. But some issues are still being debated.

Women got the right to vote in 1920.

For most of the history of the United States, people had to be at least 21 years old to vote. In 1971, the voting age was lowered to 18. At the time, the United States was at war in Vietnam. Many soldiers were 18, 19, or 20 years old. People thought it was unfair that these soldiers couldn't vote when they came home. If they could fight for their country, they should be able to vote.

a U.S. soldier in Vietnam

Young adults march for the right to vote.

It makes sense that people have to be a certain age to vote. No one thinks babies should vote! But what should the voting age be? If enough teenagers voted, they could help decide who wins a close election. Some people think this is a good thing. Other people do not.

In a few cities today, people as young as 16 can vote for the city leaders in local elections. Not many places have made this change. But maybe someday, the voting age for the whole country will change. People debate whether 16-year-olds are **mature** enough to decide on laws and leaders. They wonder if young people will make wise choices.

An Emerging Trend

A few countries have recently lowered their voting age to 16. Argentina and Brazil are two of the largest countries to do this.

There are some people who live in the United States, work hard, and pay taxes. But they are not allowed to vote. Only **citizens** are allowed to vote.

A person who moves to the United States has to go through many steps to become a citizen. First, they become a **permanent resident**. After five years, they can become a citizen. When they do, they can vote.

A group of people become U.S. citizens at a naturalization ceremony.

When George Washington was elected president, people did not have to be citizens to vote. Over time, states changed their laws. It became harder for people new to the country to vote.

Even if someone is a citizen, it might be hard to vote. For example, many citizens who were born somewhere else do not speak English. Before people can vote, they need to **register** to vote. This means filling out forms that may be in English. This might be an **obstacle** to voting. But there are laws in the United States about language support for voters, too.

A woman registers to vote.

Overseas Citizens

Some U.S. citizens have never lived in the United States. For example, if two U.S. citizens living in a different country have kids, those kids are citizens—even if they never step foot on U.S. land! So, when they turn 18, they can vote in U.S. elections.

Some citizens may not be allowed to vote. States can choose if people who have committed a **felony** can vote. Some states let felons vote even if they are in prison. Some states allow them to vote after they are out of prison. Other states make them wait a period of time or make them ask to be able to vote again.

There is a lot of debate about this. Some people say that felons do not have good judgment. They have hurt their communities. So, they think taking away their right to vote is a fair punishment. Other people disagree. They say that the right to vote is sacred. It should not be taken away because someone made a mistake.

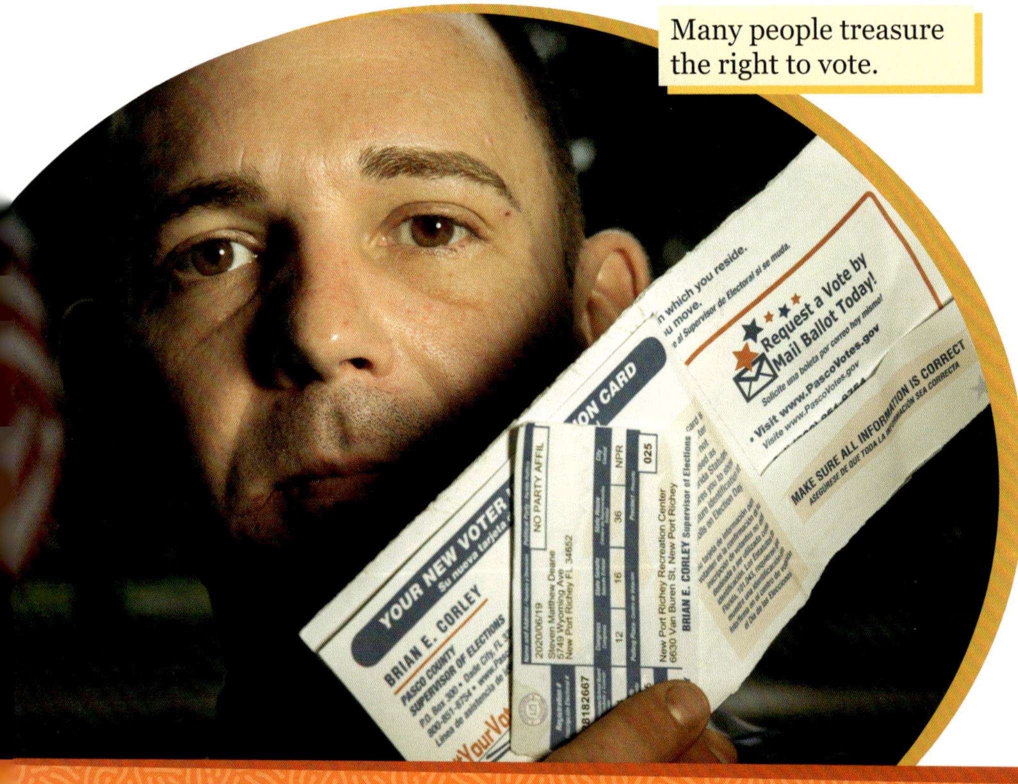

Many people treasure the right to vote.

On the List

Each state has a list of people who are able to vote. People who are able to vote still have to register to vote. If they do not register, they cannot vote until they do.

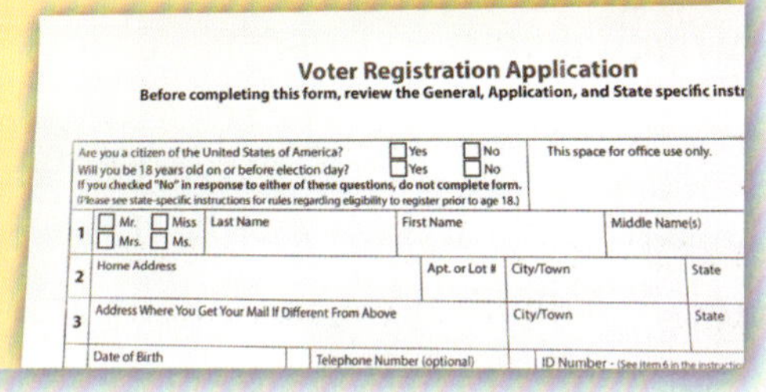
Voter Registration Application
Before completing this form, review the General, Application, and State specific instr

Are you a citizen of the United States of America? Yes No
Will you be 18 years old on or before election day? Yes No
If you checked "No" in response to either of these questions, do not complete form.
(Please see state-specific instructions for rules regarding eligibility to register prior to age 18.)
This space for office use only.

1 Mr. Miss Mrs. Ms. | Last Name | First Name | Middle Name(s)
2 Home Address | Apt. or Lot # | City/Town | State
3 Address Where You Get Your Mail If Different From Above | City/Town | State
Date of Birth | Telephone Number (optional) | ID Number

Another big debate is whether it is fair for some people to have an easier time voting than other people. In some communities, people might have to wait in line for hours to vote. Someone who lives in a different place might not have to wait at all. Many people suggest that the process of voting should be easy. Some even say that people should be able to vote online in their own homes. In many places, people can vote by mail, or they can drop off their **ballots** ahead of time.

Some people wait in very long lines to vote.

Protecting the Vote

Voting only works if the votes are counted fairly. In some countries, the people in charge control elections. They decide who counts the votes.

There are many ways to keep an election from being fair. Maybe some ballots are thrown away before they are counted. Maybe new ballots are made up that support the current leaders. Maybe the ballots are never counted at all. Instead, vote totals are made up.

In some countries and states, people need to show ID to prove they are able to vote.

These people count voter ballots.

In the United States, unfair elections either do not exist or are very rare. Many laws protect elections. Judges enforce these laws. The **free press** is important, too. Journalists can look into any voting that seems off. And if people see something strange or they do not believe the election results, they are allowed to tell everyone about it.

The United States has a tradition of honest elections. It is something to cherish. But people debate the best way to keep elections fair.

Double Up

In many elections, votes are cast using both computers and paper. This can be helpful. If the computer results are **controversial**, people can count the paper ballots.

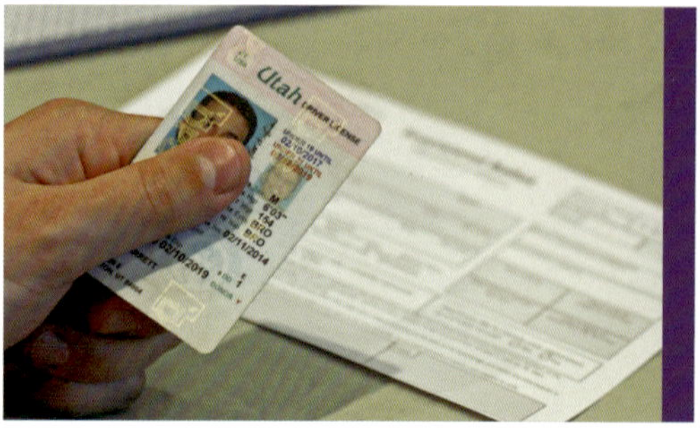

Some people worry that people who are not allowed to vote will do so anyway or that people will vote more than once. They think it is a good idea to make voters show identification (ID), such as a driver's license. They argue that this will protect the vote and that showing an ID is not a big deal.

But there is another side to this debate. There are laws already in place to make sure no one votes twice. And not everyone has a driver's license or other government ID. It costs money to get an ID. Some people might not be able to afford it.

Voters line up to get their ballots.

This machine is used to collect voter ballots.

Whether people need IDs or not does not matter if the vote is **hacked**. Computers are used to record votes and store vote totals. It is important to make sure these computers are protected. Strict efforts are used. **Securing** the vote is very important.

Think and Talk

Why is security important when it comes to voting?

Maps and Communities

Sometimes, lines on a map make a big difference when it comes to voting. In many elections, whoever gets the most votes wins. But that's not the way U.S. presidents are elected. Instead, if a candidate has the most votes from a state, in most states they get all the electors from that state. Whoever has the most electors wins. This system is called the **Electoral College**.

In some states, it is easy for a certain party to win. These states almost always vote for the candidate from that party. This means the candidates do not spend a lot of time in these states. It seems like a waste of their time when the vote is basically decided. Candidates often focus on states that are undecided or might vote in any direction. They do this to persuade voters to support them.

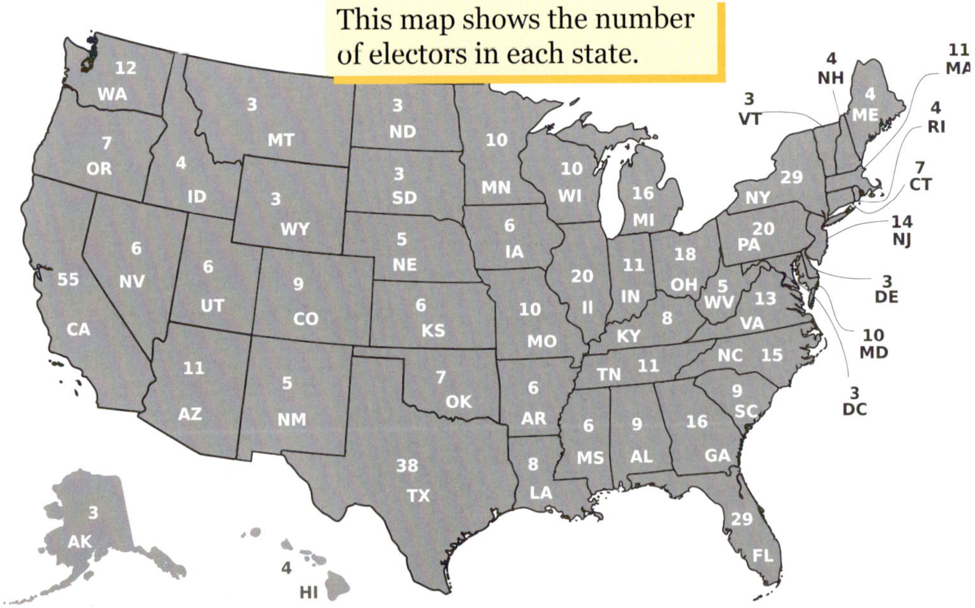

This map shows the number of electors in each state.

Congress counts the Electoral College ballots.

The system with electors has been used since George Washington's presidency. It is described in the Constitution. It is how the Founders wanted presidents chosen. There is a great deal of debate today about the Electoral College. Some people wonder if it is still the best way. Others are sure that it is. The debate goes on.

What Is It?

The Electoral College is not a school. It is a group of people who represent the vote for their home states. The voters in each state make up the popular vote for that state. But the popular vote does not decide who wins the election. The electoral vote decides. The number of electors in each state is based on that state's population. States with big populations have many electoral votes. Each state gets at least three votes.

The Constitution also created the House of Representatives. The more people who live in a state, the more representatives it has. This map shows the state of Indiana. The state has nine representatives. Some states have fewer, and some states have many more. The map is divided into nine parts. These are called **districts**. Each district votes for its own representative.

Every ten years, the district maps are redrawn. This is so that each district always has about the same number of people.

This system is as old as the country. But some people say it is not working well. The problem is that the leaders of a state can draw the lines that create the districts. They can draw lines that are fair, but they can draw lines that protect their own power, too. For example, suppose one small area in a district normally votes for a certain party. The other party may want to move that area out of the district to make it easier to win. Both parties try to make maps that are best for them.

Leaders such as these choose district boundaries.

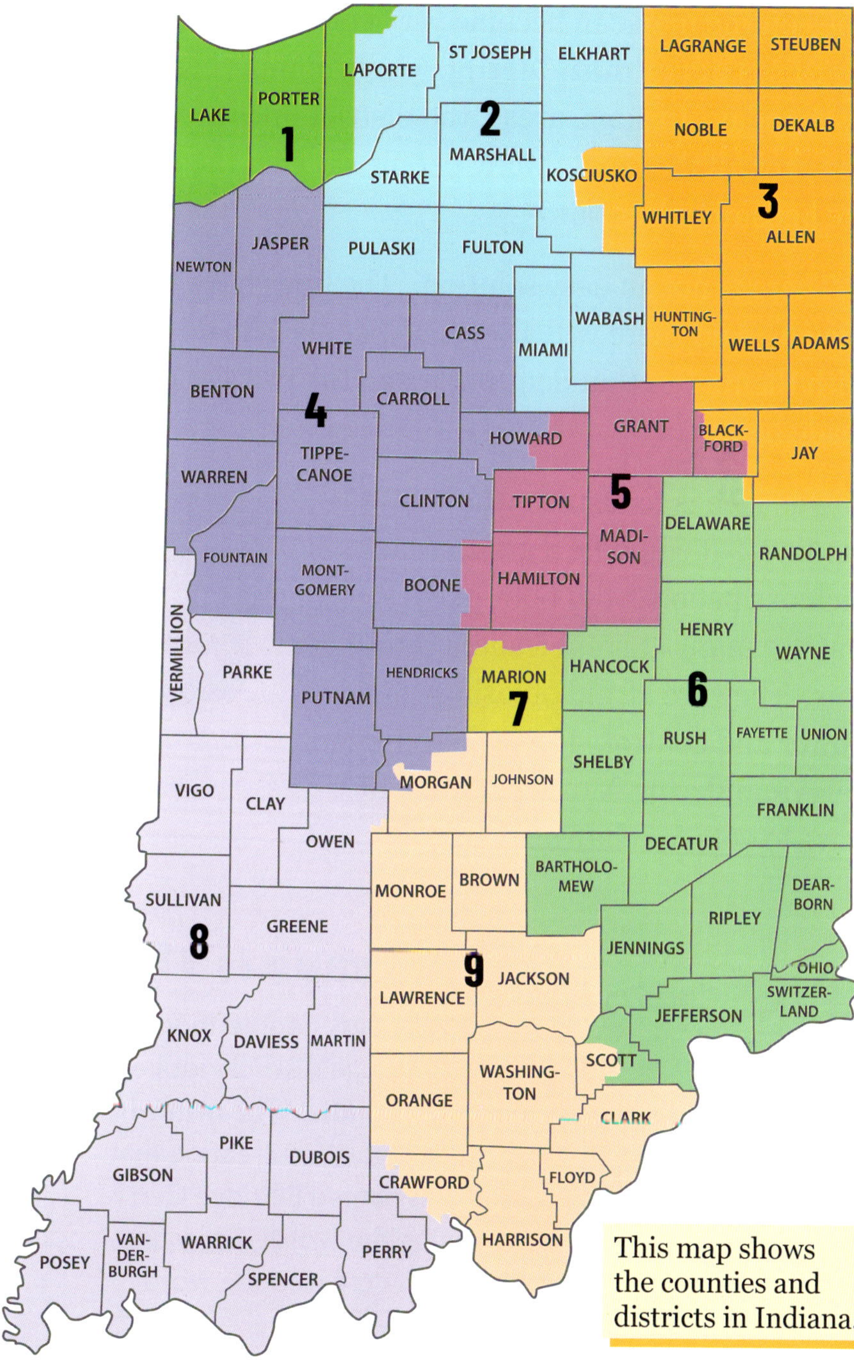

This map shows the counties and districts in Indiana.

If map creators try to give their party an advantage, the lines on the map can become very complex. The name for this is **gerrymandering**. Gerrymandering is a big issue today. In some areas, the district lines are getting stranger all the time. Many people say that the districts are becoming less fair.

There is not an easy solution. The lines have to be drawn. And there will always be people who do not agree with them. But that does not mean the process cannot be made better.

One idea is to change who draws the lines. It could be a group who includes people from both parties. But not many current leaders want this. They are afraid of losing power and control. If people think gerrymandering is unfair, they will have to vote for change.

Think and Talk

What effects might gerrymandering have on voting?

What Shape Is That?

A long time ago, people thought one of these strange districts looked like a **salamander**. The man who was responsible for creating that shape was named Elbridge Gerry. Combining the words *Gerry* and *salamander* created the word *gerrymander*.

How Gerrymandering Works

There are 20 yellow and 30 green precincts. In a majority vote, **green wins**.

There are five districts created across the precincts. In every district, **green wins** by the majority vote.

There are five gerrymandered districts across the precincts. In majority votes, **yellow wins**.

Constant Work

In the early days of voting in the United States, two candidates were listed at the top of a sheet of paper. Each person voted by signing their name under their choice.

George Washington

This system worked fine when very few people voted. But today, more than 300 million people live in the United States. More than 100 million people vote for president. A sheet of paper big enough for all those signatures would be many, many miles long.

What works today may not work in the future. Imagine a few hundred years from now. People might debate whether smart robots should be able to vote!

It is hard to know the best way to vote. It is hard to know the fairest way to vote. Elected leaders make a huge difference in everyone's life. A city might succeed with one mayor or fail under another. One president may put the country at risk. Another may make the country stronger. Voting is important work.

It is also constant work to protect voting. But it is worth the effort!

counting votes long ago

counting votes today

Glossary

amendments—changes to the U.S. Constitution

ballots—sheets of paper or tickets that are used to vote in elections

citizens—people who legally belong to a country and have its rights and protections

Constitution—the basic framework of the U.S. government

controversial—causing much disagreement

democracy—a form of government in which people vote for their leaders

differs—is different

districts—areas in a state with one representative each

Electoral College—the system used in U.S. presidential elections in which each state has a certain number of electors

felony—a major crime

free press—news media that is not controlled or restricted by the government

gerrymandering—shaping districts to benefit one party

hacked—broken into for purposes of causing harm

issues—important topics

mature—having or showing the mental and emotional qualities of an adult

obstacle—block

permanent resident—someone who lives in a country and plans to become a citizen but is not yet one

register—to officially sign up for something

salamander—a water animal that looks like a small lizard

securing—protecting and making safe

sheriffs—people in charge of law enforcement for a county

Index

Registrar of Voters
Return your ballot early!
¡Devuelva su boleta temprano!
Sobre de Devolución
acvote.org
NO POSTAGE NECESSARY IF MAILED IN THE UNITED STATES
OFFICIAL ELECTION MAIL
Official Vote by Mail Ballot
Boleta Oficial de Votación por Correo
Para ser abierto solo por la junta de escrutinio electoral
BUSINESS REPLY MAIL
FIRST-CLASS MAIL PERMIT NO. 4310 OAKLAND, CA
POSTAGE WILL BE PAID BY ADDRESSEE
Registrar of Voters
County of Alameda
PO Box 23340
Oakland CA 94623-9828

Civics in Action

Voting is important. But how do candidates win people's votes? One way is through the speeches they make. The speeches show what matters to them. They let people know why they should vote for them.

People can also give speeches about issues that are important to them. They can use those speeches to persuade other voters. You can give it a try!

1. As a class, think of an issue that matters in your community or school.
2. Decide how you feel about the issue and what you think.
3. Write a speech about the issue. In the speech, try to persuade other people to think and feel like you do.
4. Present your speech to the class. Listen to their speeches, too.
5. Did anyone's mind change because of the speeches? How about yours?